BIG
GEORGE

How a Shy Boy Became President Washington

Anne Rockwell

ILLUSTRATED BY Matt Phelan

HARCOURT, INC. ORLANDO AUSTIN NEW YORK SAN DIEGO LONDON

SELECT BIBLIOGRAPHY

Rhodehamel, John. *The Great Experiment: George Washington and the American Republic*. New Haven, CT: Yale University Press, 1998.

Flexner, James Thomas. *Washington, the Indispensable Man*. New York: New American Library, 1984.

Bobrick, Benson. *Angel in the Whirlwind: The Triumph of the American Revolution*. New York: Penguin Books, 1998.

Unger, Harlow Giles. *The Unexpected George Washington: His Private Life*. Hoboken, NJ: Wiley & Sons, 2006.

Ellis, Joseph J. *His Excellency: George Washington*. New York: Knopf, 2004.

Ketchum, Richard M. *Victory at Yorktown: The Campaign That Won the Revolution*. New York: Henry Holt, 2004.

McCullough, David. *1776*. New York: Simon & Schuster, 2005.

Washington, George. *George Washington's Rules of Civility & Decent Behavior in Company and Conversation*. N.p.: Applewood Books, 1989.

FOR THE STORY OF CINCINNATUS

Livy. *The Early History of Rome: Books I–V of the History of Rome from Its Foundations*. Translated by Audrey de Sélincourt. London: Penguin Books, 2002.

WEBSITES

National Park Service Museum Collections, "Valley Forge National Historic Park," American Revolutionary War, http://www.nps.gov/history/museum/exhibits/revwar/vafo/vafooverview.html

George Washington's Estates & Gardens, http://www.mountvernon.org/

"Yorktown Battlefield," National Park Service, U.S. Department of the Interior, http://www.nps.gov/york/index.htm

Margaret Foster, "George Washington's Office," *Preservation*, National Trust for Historic Preservation, http://www2.preservationnation.org/magazine/archives/arc_news/072403.htm

"Revolutionary War," Fraunces Tavern Museum, http://www.frauncestavernmuseum.org/war_revolutionarywar.html

"Color Guard of the Sons of the Revolution in the State of New York," Sons of the Revolution in the State of New York, http://www.sonsoftherevolution.org/Color/cg.htm

Text copyright © 2009 by Anne Rockwell

Illustrations copyright © 2009 by Matt Phelan

www.HarcourtBooks.com

Library of Congress Cataloging-in-Publication Data

Rockwell, Anne F.

Big George: how a shy boy became President Washington/Anne Rockwell; illustrated by Matt Phelan.

p.   cm.

Includes bibliographical references.

Summary: Portrays George Washington as a shy boy who wasn't afraid of anything except talking to people, but who grew up to lead an army against the British and serve as president of the new nation.

1. Washington, George, 1732–1799——Juvenile literature.   2. Presidents——United States——Biography——Juvenile literature.

[1. Washington, George, 1732–1799.   2. Presidents.]   I. Phelan, Matt, ill.   II. Title.

E312.66.R63   2009

973.4'1'092——dc21

[B]   2002004984

ISBN 978-0-15-216583-3

First edition

H G F E D C B A

Printed in Singapore

The illustrations in this book were done in pencil and gouache.

The display type was set in Algerian Mesa.

The text type was set in P22Morris.

Color separations by Colourscan Co. Pte. Ltd., Singapore

Printed and bound by Tien Wah Press, Singapore

Production supervision by Christine Witnik

Designed by April Ward

For Nicholas, Julianna, Nigel, and Christian
—A. R.

For Bob Humble, with my sincere gratitude
—M. P.

THREE HUNDRED years ago, there was no United States of America. Instead, there were thirteen English colonies in North America.

In the one called Virginia, a tall boy loved to get on his horse and gallop through the woods alone. He wasn't afraid of bears, or wolves, or the native hunters with bows and arrows who shared those woods. George Washington wasn't afraid of anything, except making conversation.

He was shy.

When George was eleven, his father died. George's
grown half brother, Lawrence Washington, became like a
father to him. At Mount Vernon, the farm where Lawrence
lived, he taught George everything a Virginia gentleman
needed to know.

Lawrence had a fine library where George read many books and especially enjoyed the stories of ancient Roman heroes. One told of a man named Cincinnatus, a Roman farmer who put down his plow to become a leader when his people called on him, and returned to the plow to become a farmer again when he was no longer needed to lead.

George practiced handwriting by copying from a book of manners. He memorized the sentences he copied, for he figured they were important. He understood that good manners could hide his shyness.

George grew taller and stronger, and he was good at sports. Besides riding horseback, he enjoyed fencing, playing ball, and firing a musket. He also liked to hunt and decided he'd one day become a brave soldier like Lawrence, who had a fine uniform and shining sword. George would be ready in case the king ever called upon him to fight.

George was also very good at drawing and mathematics. When he was sixteen, he became a surveyor and mapmaker for the king. He rode into the wilderness to measure unexplored land and draw maps of the colony.

George Washington was good at many things, but he had one big fault. He never knew what to say unless he lost his temper. Then too many angry words poured out.

George grew to be six feet three inches tall and towered over everyone around him. He loved to dance at the many balls held on neighboring farms. He didn't need to talk while fiddles played. The girls he danced with said he was the best dancer in the colony of Virginia—and the handsomest, too.

When George was nineteen, he and Lawrence sailed to Barbados, an English colony in the West Indies. They hoped that the year-round sunshine would cure Lawrence's tuberculosis. George caught smallpox and recovered. But Lawrence died shortly after they sailed home to Virginia.

George inherited Lawrence's fine uniform and sword and became the master of Mount Vernon. But he missed his brother terribly. For the rest of his life, George never spoke of that heartbreaking time.

George soon had a chance to use Lawrence's shining sword. In 1755 the king ordered him to fight French soldiers and American Indian tribesmen at Fort Duquesne, in Pennsylvania. His leader would be the English general Edward Braddock.

George knew how the American Indians fought. They hid silently behind trees, then leaped out, brandishing weapons. They usually won. French soldiers had learned to fight this way, too.

George told General Braddock he thought they should use the American Indian tactic of surprise attack. But Braddock insisted they march into battle in a long line, accompanied by a marching band to keep them in step. That was the English way.

George lost his temper. He argued with Braddock but had to give in. Young George Washington knew he had to obey his general. That was a rule of war.

The king's army lugged heavy wagons of fine food and silver tableware through the dense forest. A band marched with them, playing stirring battle songs. The silent, hidden enemies listened to the fifes and drums approaching, then leaped out from behind the trees and attacked.

Most of the king's soldiers, including General Braddock, were killed that day.

Those who survived spoke of the brave young giant who'd fought with them. His hat had been shot through and bullet holes had punctured his coat. He'd had two horses shot from under him. But George Washington was never wounded.

He didn't forget the terrible lessons of the battle now called Braddock's Defeat. He saw that real war wasn't the fun that fencing with Lawrence had been. It was tragic and bloody.

George went home to Mount Vernon with his mind made up to be a farmer for the rest of his life. He married Martha Custis, a young widow with two children.

He found farming fascinating, loving the land and what he could make it produce. And each day he galloped off on his horse to be alone in the wilderness.

Peace was better than war.

But war would come again to America. By 1775 the colonists had had enough of the many unfair laws the king of England had imposed on them. In Lexington, Massachusetts, fighting broke out between some colonists and the king's soldiers.

The colonists won. The king was angry that his soldiers had been defeated by a bunch of shopkeepers, schoolboys, and farmers. He sent more soldiers to put down this rebellion. The colonists knew they would go on fighting, and they needed a leader.

They asked George Washington to lead them. George had always been a loyal subject of the king, so it was painful to say yes. Yet he saw how the king was denying the colonists in America rights they were entitled to as Englishmen. Like Cincinnatus, the Roman farmer in the story he'd read as a boy, George knew his duty. It was to help his people fight against injustice.

So, George picked up his sword and rode off to Philadelphia, where the second Continental Congress was meeting. Farmer Washington became General Washington. This time he wouldn't be fighting for the king of England, but against him. He'd be leading an army of men and boys who'd never been soldiers.

On July 4, 1776, the Declaration of Independence was signed and read to the people. As inspiring as Thomas Jefferson's words were, George Washington knew he needed more than words to rouse the spirits of his men. Many were so sure they couldn't win, they were deserting the army and going home.

George had to make his soldiers believe in him and in themselves. He needed a military victory.

On Christmas Day in 1776, General George Washington and 2,400 soldiers were camped on the Pennsylvania side of the Delaware River. Across the river on the New Jersey side, Hessian professional soldiers from Germany, hired by the king, celebrated with good food and wine.

Late that night, while the Hessians slept, full of their feast, American soldiers silently followed General Washington onto boats. Through swirling waters filled with dangerous chunks of ice, they crossed the mighty Delaware. They surprised the Hessians and won the battle that followed.

From then on the English never knew when or where
George Washington would attack. They called him an old fox
because of his secrecy and slyness.

Luck was with him, too. In the midst of battle, he was a perfect
target, towering over everyone around him. But he was never wounded,
just as it had been during Braddock's Defeat. When smallpox broke
out in the crowded camps, George didn't catch it, for he'd been made
immune by the attack of the disease in Barbados.

But his soldiers didn't know about his immunity. They said God must be looking out for him, that General George Washington had been divinely chosen to lead them. More and more came to fight with him.

Yet as bravely as the American colonial soldiers fought against the well-trained and well-equipped English army, victory that would bring an end to the fighting eluded them.

In the winter of 1777, George Washington and his army camped at Valley Forge, Pennsylvania. Fighting had stopped. Snow lay deep on the ground. The soldiers were out of food, clothes, ammunition, and blankets. Those standing sentry left bloody footprints in the snow, for many had no shoes. Others were sick and dying, while many still well enough made their way home without permission.

Now a seasoned leader, George Washington had learned to hold his temper. All the same, no one dared disturb the general as he sat troubled and alone in his tent, the lamp burning all night. Sometimes he had a vision of victory but then feared he was dreaming. He wrote the Continental Congress, begging for shoes for his soldiers and all the other supplies they needed.

But neither shoes nor anything else came. The situation seemed hopeless.

Across the sea in Paris, Benjamin Franklin, an important American and diplomat, was trying to persuade the king of France to support the Americans. If England lost its American colonies, this would be good for France.

On the first of May, word reached George Washington that the king of France was sending guns, ammunition, uniforms, and shoes.

The miracle he'd hoped for had happened. His army was ready to fight again.

But victory was still far away.

In 1781, five thousand more French soldiers arrived in America. They were much needed. General George Washington led them south along with his American troops.

They marched to Yorktown, Virginia, where the English general Charles Cornwallis had conquered the harbor.

As soon as they reached Yorktown, George Washington picked up a shovel and started to dig. Generals usually let others do the hard labor, but George was different. His soldiers and officers joined him and continued digging through the night. By dawn a deep trench ringed the walls outside the harbor town.

It was also common for generals to stand safely on the sidelines and give orders. But not George. He picked up a musket and fired the first shot from where he stood.

The attack on Yorktown Harbor had begun.

English musket fire and cannon balls whizzed over the heads of American and French soldiers as they returned fire from the safety of their trench.

General Cornwallis hadn't expected to fight an army of this size. When he ran low on ammunition, he looked to the sea, expecting to see English ships coming to rescue him. Instead he spied ships flying the French flag. Cornwallis was trapped.

From the fort the English waved the white handkerchief that meant surrender. Eight thousand English soldiers marched peacefully toward General George Washington and lay down their guns. Their band marched behind playing a battle tune called "The World Turned Upside Down."

For it was.

The world they knew was changed forever. The long war was over, and America had won its independence.

George Washington rode to New York, where the new independent nation was making plans for peace. Many people believed the man who led them to victory should be king. But George didn't want to wear a crown. He didn't believe the new nation should be a monarchy, either. Like Cincinnatus, all he wanted was to return home to his farm and family at Mount Vernon. So he lay down his sword and said farewell to his officers and men.

But he couldn't remain a farmer. In 1789, George Washington was unanimously elected the first president of the United States of America. He didn't want the job, but he understood that to accept it was his duty. By then Americans were fighting among themselves. He knew that without a leader, everything he and his soldiers had fought for could be lost.

As history shows, President George Washington didn't let that happen. He proved to be as good a leader in peace as in war—and his leadership shaped the nation America was to become.